EULOGIES

EULOGIES

4/16/07

Bob & Cheryl –

In Remembrance of your Dad –
May Christ's Peace
abide with you & your family

J. Lukens
The Buckeye Poet

James P. Lukens

Copyright © 2003 by James P. Lukens.

Library of Congress Number: 2003092776
ISBN :   Hardcover   1-4134-0768-4
            Softcover   1-4134-0767-6

All rights reserved. No part of this book may be reproduced or transmitted in any form or by any means, electronic or mechanical, including photocopying, recording, or by any information storage and retrieval system, without permission in writing from the copyright owner.

This book was printed in the United States of America.

To order additional copies of this book, contact:
Xlibris Corporation
1-888-795-4274
www.Xlibris.com
Orders@Xlibris.com

CONTENTS

Introduction 11
A Home 13
A Tree 15
Afterglow 17
Angels 18
Another Day 20
Another Place at Our Table 21
Arizona Chasm 22
At Twilight Time 24
Aye 25
Bless'd Saints 26
Blossom Time 27
Bravehearts! 28
"Bro" 29
Bye 'n Bye 30
Canine Family Member, Friend 31
Chilled 32
Christ's Cross 33
Confession 34
Déjà vu 35
Eternal Kinship 36
"Father, Forgive Them . . ." 37
Fermentation 38
"Friends" 39
God and I 40
God Can 41
Higher Up 42
His Home 43
His Peace Be with You 44

House of Crosses	45
Humanity!	46
I Am	47
Jus' Passing Through	48
Kings	49
Laborers	50
Leaflet	51
Leaves	52
Little Sis	53
Lovin' Lover	54
Magnificat anima mea Dominum	55
Moon Mood	56
Mornin' Exercise	57
My Rose	59
Neighbor Boy	60
O Lord, I Thank Thee	61
Oh, Heavenly Breeze	62
Solar Power	63
Phantom Schooner	64
Pondering	65
Praise Christ	66
Praise the Lord!	67
Quiet Thoughts	68
" . . . Salt!"	69
Sheep!	70
Signs	71
Tenderly	72
The Breath	73
The Gift	74
The God-man	75
The Gulls	76
The Isle of St. George	77
The Lane	78
The Poet Knows	79
The Silence . . .	80
The String	81

Warrior, Father, Friend 82
Verse 83
Weeping Willow 84
White Knee Sox 85
Why? 88
Windsongs 89
Winter's Trees 90
Waves Forever 91
About the Author 93

In Remembrance

This book of poetry is a tribute to the families
who lost loved ones in America's holocaust.
On that horrific Thursday, September 11, 2001,
heroes were born and died the same day, but not in vain.
"Greater love has no one than this,
that one lay down his life for another" (St. John 15:13).
Freedom loving people everywhere must never forget the
countless selfless acts of heroism.

If freedom isn't worth dying for, life isn't worth living.
— The Author

INTRODUCTION

Writing and selecting poems of inspiration for this book has been a serious endeavor with the intent of comforting broken hearts during the mourning process.

Whether one seeks consolation through the quieting words of the beloved Twenty-third Psalm, or Saint Paul's letter to the Church at Corinth (I Corinthians 15:51), "Behold I tell you a mystery, we shall not all sleep, but we shall all be changed," herein is the great hope of the Church, that separation from loved ones is only temporal. Let us pray that hearts never ache so much or become so hardened by the sting of death that mourning cannot produce the sweet release of peace God intended for us.

A HOME

To some, "home"
is just a house,
a place to hang
their hats and coats.

To others, "home"
is "over there,"
where they get along
with other folk(s).

But to me, "home"
is far more than
just a roofed abode
built of brick
and stone or wood.

'Cause the frame of a house
is an empty shell

until it's anointed with
the joy of laughter,
tears of sorrow,
and filled with prayers
for our tomorrows.

Alas, dear friends, when
God's love abounds within
its sacred walls,
that's when our house becomes
a "Home Sweet Home" to all.

A TREE

A tree
is more than just a tree.
A tree
gives us shade
from solar heat.
T-I-M-B-E-R
There goes another tree
to serve as shelter for you and me.
My plea
to humanity of every creed,
be mindful God gave us just so many trees!
That's why we need to seed and reseed
and plant and replant a hundred million trees,
'cause, you see, a tree
is more than just a tree.
A tree is something to behold.
Some are spindly, young, and others
oh, so very old,
they die and return to earth
where they'll produce barrels and barrels
of scarce black gold.

And then again
there are skinny ones
with branches thin
and some quite short
with stocky limbs.
So it matters not
how large or small
or fat or tall,
'cause a tree is more
than just a piece of wood.
Next time we pray
or sing a hymn,
let's thank God,
for a tree is more than just a tree
growing heavenward
with outstretched limbs.

AFTERGLOW

of yellow, gold,
leaf-laden limbs
in reflective tones,
heaven's way to say
there's more to life
than we now know...
immersed, baptized
in the radiant
Afterglow.

ANGELS

There are angels walking among us;
do you feel the brush of their wings?
Now hear a whispered prayer of comfort
to ease your suffering's sting!

Yes, there are angels hovering around us,
they're God's army of sentinels strong.
So when danger or death stalks about us
plead protection from His celestial throng.

Some doubters say "seeing is believing"—
then catch a glimpse of that glorious soul,
over there by the bed of the gravely ill child—
God's healing light in the valley of woe.

Next time principalities of darkness
surround your loved ones and friends,
let your cries be known to the Father,
He'll summon His angelic beings.
Only God commands legions of angels,
He uses a stranger, a friend or a mom
to impart kindly words of encouragement
with tend'rest embraces of mercy and love.

So say to life's cynics and doubters
when a stranger they entertain:
"Be mindful of the angels amongst us,
they will send you God's heavenly sign!"

(May His guardian angels protect your home.)

ANOTHER DAY

Sunrise gives us hope,
we'll stay another day,
here among the whitewashed
birch, where we hear the river say:

"Could this be what heaven's like?
Must we wait another day?"

O river flowing by our feet,
we hear your passing message
that radiant beams of sunrise
whisper to reassure us
that heaven still awaits.

ANOTHER PLACE AT OUR TABLE

Set one more place at the table, dear,
I wonder for whom it might be?
Is it a place for Uncle Abel
or grandniece Anabelle Lee?

There's a vacant place at the table, dear,
awaiting that coveted guest.
So add more milk to the taters, Mabel,
don't waste a crumb or a crust.

Fill the plate to overflowing, dear,
to feed that very important guest,
who, of course, is heaven-blest.

ARIZONA CHASM

"Pardner, there's a chasm
in the ground in Arizona,
whose depth and breadth
our minds can never fathom."

So on faith alone let us
accept this geologic wonder
as a sculptured gift of beauty
from our Creator, God.

Traveler, if you've yet to venture
to the chasm in the ground in Arizona,
that gargantuan crevassed
stratum carved in stone,

then go stand upon its precipice
and drink in the heavenly view;
watch the "King of Canyons" stretch
across miles of solitude.
Gaze downward at the ribbon running
'cross its basement floor;
witness the mighty Colorado
chopping out what lies before.
Now you know why pilgrims trek
from every corner of the globe—
and as you listen closely to
their gasps of reverent tones—

(In a whisper they will ask)
"Arizona native, could you help us
understand this awesome geologic span?"
To which our guide replied,

"Pardner, there's no other in the land
like our Grand Canyon,"
and with humble words,
he fumbled to describe
the chasm in the ground in Arizona—
'cause it's the grandest canyon
in the world, by God's design!

AT TWILIGHT TIME

At twilight time
'tis God and I
alone as morning breaks.
At twilight time
my words come slowly
as all creation wakes.

At twilight time
in prayer I share
my private thoughts
with God, who sees clean
through my cloaked facade.

Yet He alone
loves me more,
not less
at twilight time.

AYE

Twilight is that mystical moment
between nightfall
and early dawn . . .

as black pitch gives way
to grayish light . . .
Aye
some things don't stay
black and white.

BLESS'D SAINTS

Bless'd saints have blazed the trail,
bravely, selflessly, suff'ringly frail;
martyr'd, burned and bloodied souls
embrac'd by Christ, they surround His throne,
singing, praising their sovereign Lord.

BLOSSOM TIME

Pink and white
and purple hues
of blossoms through
my window view.
'Round each twist
and bend of road,
I gasp at
Nature's canvas (awesome!)
splashed with
plum and apple blossoms.
Spring's masterpiece
of dogwoods white and
pink unfold their
flowering crosses;
symbolic of season's
reborn trees and shrubs
once more await next year's
curtain call
to inspire
travelers passing through
God's woodland paradise
at an appointed time in another life.

BRAVEHEARTS!

Distant voices gasp, then squeal
shrill alarms that waft o'er moors 'n fields.

Wee-o-wee-o, wail the pipes o' clans in plaid,
brave 'n bloodied sturdy lads.

Bravehearts never falter. They despise retreat.
Rob Roy, William Wallace, courageous martyrs these!

Kilted warriors love their freedoms,
ready to fight, to die for liberty's fresh air

'til Christ's return, Who rewards them,
aye! with eternal victory!

"BRO"

I like to call you brother,
or in jest I call you "Bro,"
but the man I can rely on
is plainly brother Joe!
Sure, you've surpassed
the living standard,
for that it makes me proud,
but man's worth
isn't measured by one's gold,
it's his heart full of compassion,
that counts with me the most,
he's my brother, he's my "Bro"!

BYE 'N BYE

Think about the days gone by
when life seemed kinder, bye 'n bye.
Cherished thoughts we share don't die,
their ghosts just linger in mind's eye.
Lush tenderness of passion's lips,
those romantic days of celestial bliss.
Tho' we've parted from that place in time,
we must not mourn should one of us die,
'Cause one day we'll embrace, in the bye 'n bye.

CANINE FAMILY MEMBER, FRIEND

Canine family member, friend,
how close to us you've grown.
A pet, a pest, a furry rug,
a loyal dog we love to hug.

Canine family member, friend,
by name you come when you are called.
Come! Dog gone, come home!
It's time to rest your velvet head.

Oh, canine family member, friend,
a bowl of gruel, bone treats await.
A lick, a nod, a wag of tail
to show your dogly love.

Oh, canine family member, friend,
from cuddly pup to old age grown.
Time to rest that weary head
in the arms of those you love.

CHILLED

Chilled by February's cutting cold
the ever-faithful farmer's wife
gives a wave "So long" to her lover
headed for the timber'd knoll
whence he stopped to lift a hand
and nod with unseen smile.

She, standing on their porch, with apron
wrapped around bare arms,
fends off the dampness in the wind,
chilled,
with shiver wipes a bittersweet tear
where once his lips impressed,
parted for awhile.

CHRIST'S CROSS

The Cross, the Cross,
the wondrous Cross,
Where Christ shed His
blood for me.

Oh, the Cross, Christ's Cross,
His marvelous Cross,
where He died to set me free.

To all who bow at His
glorious Cross,
to all who trust and obey:

When we repent of our sins
at the foot of Christ's Cross,
the victory is ours today!

CONFESSION

I heed your call
across the miles:
"Come home! Come home!"
Oh, friend of God,
keep reaching out
to heed the call,
to bow, confess.
Oh prodigal child,
put on my robe, the ring,
I'll kill the fatted calf
as saints rejoice,
"You're home at last!"

DÉJÀ VU

From some distant land
(I know not where)
my lover calls me hither
with scented breath of
Irish clover,
that wafts across those fields
of heather.

From whence I've been
(I know not when)
as in mind's eye I recollect
the tempter's taunt from
distant haunt,
yet,

(I know not where or why or when)
my lover calls me home again.

ETERNAL KINSHIP

Somehow I feel a kinship
with the soil,
the setting sun,
the brooding whippoorwill.

Sometimes I feel near
the tides of sea,
whispers of leaves on trees,
singing prayers of praise
to Thee.

But mostly,
I covet citizenship
in heaven,
where I'll have residence
in the New Jerusalem.

"FATHER, FORGIVE THEM..."

Our Father's hands are ever strong,
they lift us up when we have fallen;
are ever near when our spirit's broken.
His caring hands that shaped the world,
which loved us so much they sacrificed
His only begotten Son; then our prideful
hands through wrists did drive the spikes,
as with outstretched arms, our Christ,
thus cried: "Father, forgive them..."

FERMENTATION

Fermentation bitter, sweet,
He yearns to set us free.
Through shed blood
only martyrs know,
fermentation slakes not
the thirst of Christ
who tasted the vinegar first.

His is the way,
the life set free,
He modeled, tasted the
fermentation fee
(that we)
might join Him in eternity.

"FRIENDS"

Either we've been friends forever,
or we never have been friends.

From then 'til now—heaven knows—
our friendship'll never end.

God bless, Godspeed across the miles,
our tears, our smiles we send.

'Cause deep within, through thick 'n thin,
we'll forever be faithful friends.

GOD AND I . . .

had some time
this morn . . .

Well, really,
He was there
all along . . .

'Twas I,
not God,
who had stayed
away so long.

GOD CAN...

do anything
He pleases with me.

He can mold me
remake me, break me.

He's sovereign creator
in command.

God first loved me
world without end.

God can...
do anything. He knows the plan.

HIGHER UP

Reaching heavenward,
arms outstretched,
the army of trees stand erect
as frozen wretches trying
to escape their snowbound rootedness,
whose testaments make each season
cause célèbre
from spring's canopy,
summer's heat,
fall's painted backdrop,
winter's austere silhouette,
outstretched arms reach,
ever reaching to something higher up.

HIS HOME

When all is said and done,
when we've moved on
to a quiet, gentler place beyond,
which surely shall be heaven;
a place, a home of poetic thoughts
the psalmist sings to us about
let us prepare our yearning souls
to join the heavenly throngs
who've gone on before, given in to Him
their hearts, their brains, sinew and blood,
in turn He'll fill their space with love,
for He is a tender, merciful Father, God.

HIS PEACE BE WITH YOU

Without the great I AM,
the comforter,
one could not bear the burden.

Now, may His mercy
be sufficient unto you
throughout each day.

I pray, the peace of Christ
reigns within your heart
until the grand reunion day.

HOUSE OF CROSSES

Bearing scars, those hardwood doors
on which His cross appears
is a testament of His sacrifice,
the Christ who vanquished fear
of death, a reminder, yes,
on every door within our house,
where once I was blind, but now I see,
I once was lost, but now I'm found,
Oh, House of Crosses, your every door
bears the sacred symbol saints adore.
A reminder of His death for us,
thanks be to God our house is blest!

HUMANITY!

Humanity, humanity!
What a hocus-pocus crowd.

You stake your claim on vanity,
your solemn oaths, how proud!

Is not there more to life, you dandy?
Is it simply when you die, you die?

My God will not forsake your pride,
your thirst He's sure to slake.

Just repent, repent! abide! abide!
or suffer the eternal wake.

I AM

Who goes there at the edge of
day's glow?

Listen! Be still my soul to hear
the howl
that chills my blood!

Out! Evil shadow I shudder
at the thought
as death's thief lurks to steal
me away.

yet another voice from deep within
reveals Him,
who knows no sin.
(Who knows my sin.)

Salvation's Word! I belong to Him,
a child of His,
the great I AM.

JUS' PASSING THROUGH

Hear the mellow metal chimes
of Maine announcing

in the blowing wind that I'm
jus' passing through

each time a welcome breeze
doth whisper to you

know it's your mate, your friend,
beckoning to come in

before the stillness steals
me away again.

KINGS

Kings of the present
are we

no promise of tomorrow
today.

Kings of the present
are we

our travels are near,
never far.

Kings of the present
are we,

we learned from
the past

to save the best
for last.

Kings of the present
are we.

LABORERS

Farmers in the fields must toil
as wives faithfully carry their pails
while these proud laborers mow their hay
through moonlit night and dust of day.

Their eyes glance skyward at high noon
to see crows bound for lunch in town,
where stone masons wield their leaden tools,
the trowels that cement foundation stones
of houses, churches, and red-brick schools.

Let us salute the laborers in the fields and towns,
for work is toil when sweat's on brows
no matter who or where or how
their salty drips stain shirt and ground.

Alas, the laborers' work is never done
'til the jobless folks do ask to till
the fields and carry the pails
and wield the trowels to give rest
to those who've done their best—
as we all make the most
of the time that's left!

LEAFLET

Leaflet, leaflet,
a thing unique,
whose vein-lined hand
waves in the breeze.
Leaflet, leaflet
adorns each tree,
from birth of seed
'til winter's deed.
Leaflet, leaflet,
lest I ignore a leafless limb,
I'm inspired by God
to pen spring's hymn.

LEAVES

Yellow, crimson, crinkled brown,
leaves float lazily to ground
as each day a seasoned soul goes home,
flies heavenward to God.

As grains of hourglass sand keep time,
the counting, mounting reminder signs
that mortal lives like leaves on trees
must join death's silent symphony.

LITTLE SIS

She was with us as a whisper,
but a wisp of summer's breeze,
this little sis, our little sister,
an ever free and playful she.

Her eyes of Irish a-smilin'
could thaw out the coldest hearts;
then without a moment's notice
God set her apart.

O'er the years we miss her,
we still feel the mourning pain,
of that lovely little sister,
our loss,
but heaven's gain.

LOVIN' LOVER

Everybody needs a little lovin',
everybody needs a lot of love
but me,
'cause I'm overflowing with your love,
your everlovin' love for me.

MAGNIFICAT ANIMA MEA DOMINUM

Holy Mary full of grace,
purest virgin, ever chaste.

Righteous lady, who gave birth
to holy child, the Prince of Peace.

Whose holy Son, the Three in One,
bore our sins upon the tree

as Holy mother, exalts her Son:
"My soul magnifies Thee!"

MOON MOOD

A sliver of moon
like a slice of orange
beams a wisp of light
in the cloudless night.

Through narrow window
of quiet room,
I ponder the message
of the lunar mood.

MORNIN' EXERCISE

Have you listened lately, friend,
early in the mornin'
when the sun
begins to rise?
Do you hear the neighbor's rooster crowin'
as you wipe the stardust from your eyes
and stretch your arms to heaven,
yawn and do your mornin' exercise?
Have you listened in the mornin'
when the sun begins to rise
to the neighbor's baby cryin',
cryin' out its baby cries;
while the wife's a-fryin' eggs 'n bacon
and the world comes back to life—
as you stretch your limbs to ceilin'
and start your mornin' exercise?

Now if you listen closely, friend,
early in the mornin'
you can hear the murmur of a prayer
from the little church 'round the corner.
First, it starts out kind-a lowly,
then it begins to grow
as the preacher and his breth'ren
are prayin' penance to a righteous, holy God.
Early in the mornin'
as the sun begins to rise,
if you listen closely, friend,
you can hear the saints
a-doin' their mornin' exercise!

MY ROSE

My Rose in a vase
whose pretty face
with folded smiles
thine scented breath
tempts many a nose
to your repose
atop thorned stem
where prick offends.
Your love must wear
a garden glove
on rendezvous
with rosey bud
should one be called
to lift her bloom
from long-stemmed
vase to tomb.

NEIGHBOR BOY

Neighbor boy has gone to be
with Jesus Christ of Galilee.
Tears are shed by kin and friends,
their sorrowful loss is heaven's gain.

This lad knew love and gave it well
to wife and child, his mother tells.
In sleep she weeps her son's departing
as angels mend her broken heartstrings.

Dear saints keep faith as others leave
to be with Christ of Galilee,
who prepares each heart with Eternal Peace
to ease death's sting of our beloved deceased.

O LORD, I THANK THEE

O Lord, I thank Thee
for the scented air
upon the breeze,
as each change of season

ordains the air I breathe
for which, O Lord,
I become refreshed, renewed,
made whole again,

O Lord, I thank Thee.

OH, HEAVENLY BREEZE

Oh, heavenly breeze,
we hear ya
whisperin' to us
through the leaves.

Where d'ya come from
and where are ya goin'?
Oh, heavenly breeze,
is it really worth knowin'?

You'll often forewarn us
before the dark storm
with deathly stillness,
calmest of the calm.

Then, right after the torrent,
your breath becomes fresh
when once again ya
whisper to us—
"I just came from heaven!"

SOLAR POWER

Sol with raiment
gold and orange
strolls across
the summer dome.

Darth Vadar night
shrinks, then dies,
as Mother Earth rolls
on her side.

Old Sol is on the rise again,
over the crest of the applewood,
his rays shine forth to brighten
our way, our mood within,

to behold daybreak
the way we should!

PHANTOM SCHOONER

Ghostly sails appear through shroud
of ocean mist whose clouds
conceal the waves of minions
through fog-laced veil (this side of theirs)
the Captain's voice invites us:
"All Aboard!"
Now we set sail to the other side,
the heavenly realm beyond this world.

PONDERING

In the pasture is a pond
so crystal clear that
I am fond to look upon
and see a face I know.

The face I see is not at all
the one I saw before ripples
caused by darting dragonfly
distorted nose and squinted eyes
to half their size.

On daily treks to land-locked pool
where summer bliss awaits,
I love to sip its nectar cool
and contemplate:
"How diff'rent life might look to me
if I had the face I see
before the pond was ripple-free."

PRAISE CHRIST

Wellsprings flood my soul,
as cups of grace doth overflow.

Praise Christ, who quenches our thirst,
to give my life, and yours, new worth.

PRAISE THE LORD!

Praise the Lord, my God,
my Savior and my King.

Praise the Lord, my God,
I thank Him for everything!

Praise the Lord on high,
to Him my soul does sing.

Praise the Lord, hallelujah!
Won't you make Him your
King of kings?

Praise the Lord, our God,
our King of everything!

QUIET THOUGHTS

Thank you, Lord,
for the solitude
of morning in
the quietude of day
that only you can bring.

We praise you, Lord,
for the hush, the peace,
how comforting, as we
listen closely
to the flap of angels'
wings in heaven.

"... SALT!"

(St. Matthew 5:13 NAS)

Together we say at sup:
"Please pass the salt, the salt!"
Without the loyal covenant salt,
there is no seasoned table talk.

Salt to heal the thoughtless acts,
so heed the ever sacred pact
to pass the loyal covenant salt
shared at the feast among God's folk,
whose enemies are powerless to provoke.

In remembrance of the spoken oath,
whenever we gather with family folk,
say then:

"Please pass the salt, the precious salt!"

SHEEP!

Sheep! How dumb,
they're lost, 'til found.

Their wool o'er eyes,
they plod along,

confused, forlorn
until they're shorn

by the Good Shepherd,
who kindly, gently . . .

leads them home . . .

SIGNS

Late summer signs are all around,
they usher in the autumn sounds,
as locusts serenade tree frogs,
morning sun burns off ground fog,
as we huddle near dying campfire,
too soon comes cold to quench desires.

TENDERLY

You left, we parted tenderly,
my bride,
every moment we cherished,
we held, we now hold in memory,
my love,
precious thoughts of each other,
dear one,
tenderly in thought we hold the other,
my lover,
ever, always our heart's desire,
we know we'll be together . . .
always.

THE BREATH

A breath of summer came

to visit us

through the screen that strains

out soot and moth,

yet filters not the scent of fresh

mown grass

or fumes that delight

of mem'ries past,

whose fragrance lasts

'til it evaporates

as we breathe in our last

euphoric gasps.

THE GIFT

In shadows of dying dusk
leafy canopies, so lush,
'gainst my windowpanes do brush
to remind me of the gift, the hush,
of summer eves we love so much
beneath the trees to cuddle up,
to savor the gift, the greenery, so plush,
in fading shadows of dying dusk.

THE GOD-MAN

Sharper than the two-edged sword,
the Word made flesh
became our King, our Lord,
since He vanquished death.

O'er past years
brave hearts conquered fear
at liberty's tree whence
the God-man passed the test.

He's the victor over evil's pride
that enslaves the patriot,
His, the ultimate sacrifice
freed from the tyrant's quest.

Die to self!
Be filled with Christ!
He, who breathes Truth alive
the only Way to eternal life.

THE GULLS

The gulls know something we
know not,
those acrobats who glide aloft.

Hovering o'er rock-strewn shores
or dining on nature's
salad bar;

gulls with mates do love to play,
or soar toward
another day,

'cause gulls look down upon
the human lot,
content to know what
we do not.

THE ISLE OF ST. GEORGE

In all the world there's only one,
an island haven in the sun.

White-washed beaches lush with shells
and crabs and gulls as dolphins play
in ocean's spray . . .

Waves roll foam across our feet
to give relief from summer's heat,
'til setting sun paints clouds aloft
with salmon skies across the Gulf.

When we embrace at midnight watch,
atop the fabled widow's walk,
bright stars appear within our reach
as we witness moon's full-faced retreat.

Then,
(we toast our friends with grateful words,
that thank our Lord for dear Saint George!)

THE LANE

A virgin lane wound through
the wood.
I wondered where it stopped,
or ever would.
How tempting the lonely path
did seem,
a-ramblin' o'er flowery knoll,
among the trees.
Aye, as the poet pondered the road
to take,
the virgin lane I chose not, ne'er to
forsake.

THE POET KNOWS

What is it that the poet knows,
who travels life's uncertain road?
Imagine the wilderness our lives
might be,
devoid the churchyard elegy.

Is it the poet's verse, sweet verse
of painted sunsets, idyllic woods
that speak volumes to us as Psalms?
Or of tear-stained words that comfort
lonely lives with song?

Of all the messages the heart conceives,
the greatest gift the poet knows—
not that thoughts must rhyme—
but to speak the truth in love.

THE SILENCE...

In the quiet of the room
not another soul nor sound
is heard except the silence...

the stillness of another world
passing through the nothingness
that sedates the somber mood...

of a brooding heart a-beating,
beating out its sacred tune
of mem'ries past reborn...

once more the silent, quiet room,
becomes the hoped-for joyful mansion
eons... eons from the doomed.

THE STRING

Bleak, the bleakest clouds hovered
as some mysterious shroud.
Then, peeking through the grayish
bleakness was this solitary beam.
At first, a strand, a thread of lightness,
this faint brightness seemed devoured
in darkness, until a golden string
became a bolt, a rod of boldness
that parted heaven's leaden yoke;
symbolic of a God not easily provoked.

WARRIOR, FATHER, FRIEND

Oh brave, but kindly warrior,
you've fought the last good fight,
you've paid forward to help others,
you've taught us wrong from right.

With tears that cloud our eyes, friend,
we part you for a season,
we say our long "goodbyes"
knowing God rests you for a reason

as loved ones on the other side
greet your puckish grin,
we hear our kindly father sing
this, his final hymn:

"Abide, abide brave warriors . . . until we meet again."

VERSE

Poets inspired by apparitions
of mystical visions, into the dark,
lonely night they write their thoughts.

Those bards, who compose lyric verse,
into wee hours their minds traverse;
to create words that cast a spell
of loathsome plots they'd rather not tell.

Yea! their God alone, who knows best,
commands them to humbly bow, confess.
Honest poets sweat words, works of verse,
that humankind oft misinterprets.

Yet, the purist words to pour forth
from poetic souls of greatest worth
were written by poets of inspired verse.

WEEPING WILLOW...

Weeping willow tree

whose limbs droop earthward

extended in mourning pose,

alone,

a silent witness

of nature's tearful splendor,

bending forward, bowing ever lower,

how lovely is your graceful form,

the sad reminder of being true to thyself,

alone.

WHITE KNEE SOX

Out-a thin air came a woman wearin' white knee sox,
betwixt two mangy critters sportin' stockin' caps.
These somethings from another time in life,
appeared mean-spirited, low-life types.

All eyes fixed upon her escorts,
who stomped across the floor,
as the woman with white knee sox
seemed to hover,
kind-a floated through the screen door,
headed to my table, where she stopped.

Though the atmosphere was humid,
heavy as a muddy mop,
her guerrillas sat at the counter
demandin' steamin' slop.
(Ya see, the devil's agents could endure
the tropic's heat,
as the woman slid white knee sox from her filthy feet.)

Da plot began to thicken as the cook
scraped clean the pot:
"Hey, you sinner woman,
join us kneeling on the floor,
it's time for a revival before someone
gets half-crocked."
He smiled, gave her a motion,
but she hurried out the door.

The cook saved two motley strangers,
by servin' up the Word,
then sent 'em out to find the woman,
to share the bread of life,
'cause her days were numbered
and eternity's a long, long time,
(my God loves saved sinners
washed in the precious blood).

Terror gripped the cook,
who knew she'd not been fed
as she walked in stained white knee sox
among the living dead.
He prayed: "Converted partners,
find her b'fore it's too late,
'cause I have a free meal ticket,
to spare her hell-filled plate."

As the cook headed for the exit,
the door opened just a crack.
The wind blew in the woman, broken and distraught.
She hovered, kind-a floated to my table,
then she stopped.
'Twas now my time to witness:
"Your dinner plate is paid for,
just accept His saving grace.
Once you dined with sinners! come!
join the banquet feast!"

WHY?

O Lord Jesus,
forgive my angry ways.
Why?
do I do the things I do
and say the things I say?
Forgive me,
Lord,
for my harsh tirades,
before sunset of another
precious day!

WINDSONGS . . .

(Dedicated to our moms
and mothers everywhere.)

Windsongs whisper in our ears
the gentle hums of yesteryears,
when Mama held us at her side
singin' lovely lullabies.

Her voice as angel's bell doth ring
with tenderness to us she'd sing,
homey mem'ries windsongs inspire
as she's joined God's Heav'nly choir.

WINTER'S TREES

This eve through windowpanes
(I see)
the bony branches bare of leaves,
the limbs stark, old, so cold;
which causes me to bemoan what
once was green with gene of life
now represents some helpless form
that's given up, that's died,
yet hope of hope I have, I hold
for spring,
when at the fingertips of trees
(I see)
a bud, a bloom I've come to know
as heaven's sign that new life
returns to winter's trees.

WAVES FOREVER

O, wave to us Old Glory
to remind us of your story
of those who shed their blood,
our heroes of Nationhood.

O, wave to us Old Glory,
tell the red, white, blue story
brave souls of freedom's dream,
not one ever died in vain.

We salute your wave Old Glory,
your theme... our cause... together,
we recite:
"one nation under God,"
shall be our pledge forever.

ABOUT THE AUTHOR

At the young age of seventeen, James Lukens started his career as a writer. He has held numerous account executive-copywriting positions with advertising and public relation firms. In more recent years, he's enjoyed freelance writing as a hobby. The diversity of his writing assignments range from the technical to such mundane items as garden hand tools.

Lukens' books, Heart Thoughts and "Windowpanes," have been added to libraries throughout his home state of Ohio. He is also among authors and poets celebrated by the Ohioana Library Association, having his books added to the state's archives. Lukens was especially honored to have his first collection added to The Royal Collection Trust housed at Windsor Castle in England.

Poet Lukens' latest collection of devotional poetry is concise and elegant. One Ohio governor said the simple joys of living found in Luken's poetry had earned him the right to be called "The Buckeye Poet." For certain, Eulogies is an affirmation of God's love for humanity that resonates with wonder and joy.